Writing Practical English 1

second edition

Writing Practical English 1

second edition

TIM HARRIS

Illustrated by **ALLAN ROWE**

HARCOURT BRACE JOVANOVICH, PUBLISHERS

SAN DIEGO   NEW YORK   CHICAGO   AUSTIN
LONDON   SYDNEY   TORONTO

ISBN: 0-15-570915-1

Library of Congress Catalog Card Number: 85-81762

Printed in the United States of America

A NOTE TO THE INSTRUCTOR

The lessons in *Writing Practical English 1,* Second Edition, are closely coordinated with the lessons in the accompanying text, *Practical English 1,* Second Edition. They provide additional writing practice using the same grammatical items. Exercises from this workbook should be assigned only after the corresponding material in the text has been covered in class. A few vocabulary items are used here before they appear in the text, but the meanings of these words are always made clear by the accompanying illustrations.

It is generally a good idea for instructors to go over the workbook exercises orally in class before assigning them as homework. This applies particularly to the picture compositions. Instructors should have students discuss a given picture in class before asking them to write a composition about it. Instructors should also explain any unfamiliar vocabulary that the students will need to know in writing their compositions.

CONTENTS

CHAPTER ONE

TO BE

Who	's (is)	this? that?

It	's (is)	Jimmy. Linda.

What	's (is)	he? she?

He She	's (is)	a student.

a *Look at the pictures and answer the following questions.*

1. Maria Miranda/doctor

Who's this? *It's Maria Miranda.*

What is she? *She's a doctor.*

2. Peter Smith/businessman

Who's this? _____

What is he? _____

3. Anne Jones/secretary

Who's this? _____

What is she? _____

4. Mr. Bascomb/banker

Who's this? _____

What is he? _____

4

5. Mrs. Golo/teacher

Who's this? _____

What is she? _____

6. Nick Vitakis/mechanic

Who's this? _____

What is he? _____

7. Ula Hackey/movie star

Who's this? _____

What is she? _____

8. Otis Jackson/artist

Who's this? _____

What is he? _____

9. Nancy Paine/pilot

Who's this? _____

What is she? _____

TO BE Affirmative

He She It	's (is)	a student. a teacher. a book.

Negative

He She It	isn't (is not)	a student. a teacher. a book.

He She It	's (is)	in the office.

He She It	isn't (is not)	in the office.

b *Write negative and affirmative statements about each picture.*

1. Maria/movie star *Maria isn't a movie star.*

   She/doctor *She's a doctor.*

2. She/home *She isn't at home.*

   She/hospital *She's at the hospital.*

3. Peter/mechanic _____

   He/businessman _____

4. He/garage _____

   He/office _____

5. Anne/student _____

   She/secretary _____

6. She/school _____

   She/post office _____

7. Tino/banker _____

   He/waiter _____

8. He/bank _____

   He/restaurant _____

6

9. Otis/businessman _____

   He/artist _____

10. He/office _____

    He/museum _____

11. Nancy/secretary _____

    She/pilot _____

12. She/office _____

    She/airport _____

13. Ula/teacher _____

    She/movie star _____

14. She/school _____

    She/movies _____

15. Mr. Bascomb/artist _____

    He/banker _____

16. He/home _____

    He/bank _____

17. Nick/pilot _____

    He/mechanic _____

18. He/airport _____

    He/garage _____

TO BE Affirmative

He She It	's (is)	at the garage.

Interrogative

Is	he she it	at the garage?

c *Make questions as indicated.*

Example: Maria is a doctor. (at the hospital)

Is she at the hospital ? _____

1. Nick is a mechanic. (at the garage)

   _____

2. Nancy is a pilot. (at the airport)

   _____

3. Mr. Bascomb is a banker. (at the bank)

   _____

4. Otis is an artist. (at home)

   _____

5. Linda is a student. (at the university)

   _____

6. Peter is a businessman. (at the office)

   _____

7. Mrs. Golo is a teacher. (at school)

   _____

8. Tino is a waiter. (at the restaurant)

   _____

9. Anne is a secretary. (at the office)

   _____

10. Ula Hackey is a movie star. (at home)

   _____

8

d *Write a sentence for each picture using the correct preposition.*

1. The book is (on/under) the chair.

The book is on the chair.

2. The flower is (next to/in) the vase.

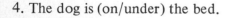

3. The magazine is (next to/behind) the clock.

4. The dog is (on/under) the bed.

5. The cat is (in front of/behind) the bird.

6. Anne is (at/in) the post office.

e   *Look at the pictures and write sentences using **this** or **that**.*

1. *This is a hat.* _____

2. *That is a glass.* _____

3. _____

4. _____

5. _____

6. _____

7. _____

8. _____

9. _____

10. _____

10

f   *Look at the pictures and write sentences using **these** or **those**.*

1. *These are flowers.*

2. *Those are apples.*

3. _____

4. _____

5. _____

6. _____

7. _____

8. _____

9. _____

10. _____

CHAPTER TWO

"To be" with
adjective

"To be" with
adjective and
noun

Singular and plural
nouns

Numbers 1–20

Time

a   *Look at the pictures and write a true sentence for each one.*

14

b *Look at the pictures and write a true statement for each one, using the adjectives* **old**, **fat**, **short**, **weak**, **young**, **tall**, **strong**, *or* **thin**.

YES/NO Question		
Is	he she it	old?

Short Answers

Yes,	he she it	is.

No,	he she it	isn't.

c *Look at the pictures and answer the questions.*

1. Is Peter married?

No, he isn't. He's single.

2. Is he happy?

Yes, he is.

3. Is Mr. Bascomb rich?

_____

4. Is he tall?

_____

5 Is Albert old?

_____

6. Is he fat?

_____

7. Is Ula Hackey short?

_____

8. Is she beautiful?

_____

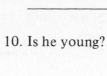

9. Is Dr. Pasto intelligent?

_____

10. Is he young?

_____

11. Is Mrs. Brown married?

_____

12. Is she thin?

_____

13. Is Jack rich?

_____

14. Is he sad?

_____

15. Is that man young?

_____

16. Is he strong?

_____

17. Is Paris an old city?

_____

18. Is Paris hot in December?

_____

TO BE Affirmative

He She It	's (is)	strong.
I	'm (am)	
You We They	're (are)	

d *Rewrite the following sentences using the pronouns **he, she, it, we,** or **they**.*

Example: Nancy is a pilot. *She's a pilot.* _____

1. Nick is a mechanic. _____

2. Nick and I are at the garage. _____

3. The garage is on Maple Street. _____

4. Mr. and Mrs. Golo are at home. _____

5. Mrs. Golo is a teacher. _____

6. Mr. Golo is a businessman. _____

7. My friends are at the art museum. _____

8. The art museum is very interesting. _____

9. The paintings are beautiful. _____

e *Complete the following sentences with the correct form of the verb **to be**.*

Example: Tino _____*is*_____ a waiter.

1. He _____ my friend.

2. I _____ a businessman.

3. My name _____ Peter.

4. We _____ at the Martinoli Restaurant.

5. Barbara _____ here.

6. She _____ with Tino.

7. They _____ next to the window.

8. This _____ a beautiful restaurant.

9. The tables and chairs _____ very old.

10. They _____ from Italy.

18

TO BE   Negative

He She It	isn't (is not)	strong.
I	'm not (am not)	
We You They	aren't (are not)	

Interrogative

Is	he she it	strong?
Am	I	
Are	you we they	

f *Make negative sentences as indicated.*

Example: He's a banker. (a doctor) *He isn't a doctor.*

1. She's a secretary. (a teacher) _____

2. They're at the office. (at home) _____

3. We're on Lime Street. (on Main Street) _____

4. It's hot today. (cold) _____

5. I'm thirsty. (hungry) _____

6. Barbara and Tino are at home. (at work) _____

7. She's beautiful. (ugly) _____

8. He's tall. (short) _____

9. They're single. (married) _____

g *Change the following sentences to the interrogative.*

Example: We're at the airport. *Are we at the airport?*

1. Those men are tourists. _____

2. They're from Brazil. _____

3. That woman is from Japan. _____

4. It's a beautiful country. _____

5. Tokyo is the capital. _____

6. You're from Canada. _____

7. Your home is in Montreal. _____

h *Complete the dialogue.*

1. *Who's* _____ that man?

2. _____ Roberto Cruz.

3. _____ very tall. _____ a basketball player?

4. No, _____. _____ a pilot.

5. _____ Roberto a Mexican?

6. Yes, _____.

7. _____ from Guadalajara?

8. No, _____.

9. What city _____?

10. _____ Mexico City.

11. _____ that the capital of Mexico?

12. _____, _____.

i *Rewrite the following sentences without contractions.*

Example: He's a pilot. *He is a pilot.* _____

1. They're mechanics. _____

2. She's at the post office. _____

3. You're a secretary. _____

4. I'm a student. _____

5. That's a good clock. _____

6. We're at home. _____

7. They're at the movies. _____

8. He's a banker. _____

9. It's an old table. _____

20

j *Change the following sentences as indicated.*

Example: That's a famous university. *That university is famous.*

1. These are beautiful flowers. _____

2. This is an expensive vase. _____

3. That's an interesting book. _____

4. Those are strong men. _____

5. These are good apples. _____

6. Those are bad oranges. _____

7. That's an old television. _____

8. This is a small hat. _____

9. That's an ugly dog. _____

k *Change the following sentences from singular to plural.*

Examples: This magazine is interesting. *These magazines are interesting.*

That's a beautiful hat. *Those are beautiful hats.*

1. That book is expensive. _____

2. This orange is good. _____

3. That's a German car. _____

4. That clock is old. _____

5. This is a cheap coat. _____

6. That's a small table. _____

7. This bottle is clean. _____

8. This is a beautiful chair. _____

9. That's an English newspaper. _____

I What time is it?

1.

It's ten o'clock.

2.

3.

4.

5.

6.

7.

8.

9.

10.

11.

12.

CHAPTER THREE

a *Look at the pictures and write a command for each one.*

1. Pay

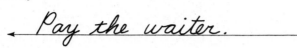

2. Call

_____→

3. Close

←_____

4. Look at

_____→

5. Open

←_____

6. Take

_____→

7. Read

←_____

8. Eat

_____→

9. Play

←_____

10. Light

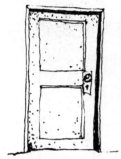

26

IMPERATIVE

Look at	Anne. Mr. Bascomb. Otis and Gloria. Barney and me. the magazine.

With Object Pronouns

Look at	her. him. them. us. it.

b *Rewrite the following sentences using object pronouns.*

1. Look at Peter and Sandy.

Look at them.

2. Come and sit with Johnnie and me.

_____→

3. Wait for Nancy.

←_____

4. Dance with Albert.

_____→

5. Please open this bottle.

←_____

6. Wash the dishes.

_____→

c *Rewrite the following sentences using object pronouns.*

Example: Come with Johnnie and me. *Come with us.* _____

1. Call Mr. Bascomb. _____

2. Listen to your friends. _____

3. Take the chair. _____

4. Wait for Nancy and me. _____

5. Talk to Linda. _____

6. Ask Mr. Field. _____

7. Look at those girls. _____

8. Read this magazine. _____

9. Dance with Maria. _____

Example: Give Peter this book. *Give him this book.* _____

1. Take Mrs. Golo the table. _____

2. Bring Linda and me the magazines. _____

3. Take Albert that letter. _____

4. Give the dog a ball. _____

5. Bring Nancy a cup of coffee. _____

6. Give your friends the oranges. _____

7. Bring Barney and me a sandwich. _____

8. Take Mr. Bascomb the newspaper. _____

9. Give Mr. and Mrs. Brown that picture. _____

28

d *Look at the pictures and write a command for each one.*

1. <u>Open the bottle.</u>

2. _____

3. _____

4. _____

5. _____

6. _____

7. _____

8. _____

9. _____

10. _____

e *Look at the pictures and answer the following questions.*

1. How old is the car?

   It's forty years old.

   How much is it?

   It's nine hundred and ninety-eight dollars.

2. How old is the record player?

   _____

   How much is it?

   _____

3. How old is the lamp?

   _____

   How much is it?

   _____

4. How old is the camera?

   _____

   How much is it?

   _____

5. How old is the bicycle?

   _____

   How much is it?

   _____

6. How old is the stove?

    _____

    How much is it?

    _____

7. How old is the vase?

    _____

    How much is it?

    _____

8. How old is the telephone?

    _____

    How much is it?

    _____

9. How old is the typewriter?

    _____

    How much is it?

    _____

10. How old is the bed?

    _____

    How much is it?

    _____

f *Ask and answer questions about the picture using the prepositions* ***in, on, next to, in front of, behind,*** *or* ***under.***

Examples: apples/ground *Where are the apples? They're on the ground.*

flowers/window *Where are the flowers? They're in the window.*

1. women/men _____

2. men/women _____

3. birds/tree _____

4. girls/tree _____

5. cats/newspaper _____

6. bicycles/house _____

7. cars/garage _____

g *Write the following words in the blanks below according to their s sound.*

watches	oranges	mechanics	books
lamps	students	buses	candles
beds	exercises	trucks	glasses
tables	envelopes	cars	windows
chairs	magazines	hats	apples
dishes	pilots	dresses	sandwiches

clocks (s)	**flowers (z)**	**vases (iz)**
lamps	*beds*	*watches*

h *Underline the stressed vowels.*

Example: expens<u>i</u>ve

telephone	hospital	dangerous	newspaper
mechanic	magazine	interesting	guitar
garage	university	museum	restaurant
library	beautiful	secretary	umbrella
department	American	nationality	intelligent

CHAPTER FOUR

Review

a *Look at the pictures and write a suitable command for each one from the list below. Use each command only once.*

Give her the flowers.   Go to her.   Come in.

Sit down on the sofa.   Take her hand.   Put the flowers in the vase.

36

Take her in your arms.　　Now get up and leave.　　Don't laugh.
Look into her eyes.　　　Close your eyes.　　　　Kiss her.

7.

8.

9.

10.

11.

12.

b *Answer the following questions.*

1. Are Romeo and Juliet happy in this scene? _____

2. Describe Romeo. Is he short and fat? _____

3. Is Juliet old and ugly? _____

4. Are Romeo and Juliet Spanish or Italian? _____

5. Who is the author of <u>Romeo and Juliet</u>? _____

6. Is <u>Romeo and Juliet</u> an opera or a play? _____

7. What's your favorite play? opera? _____

8. Who's your favorite author? _____

9. Is Shakespeare English or American? _____

c *Complete the following questions as indicated.*

Examples: That isn't Romeo. Who *is it?* _____

Juliet isn't in the garden. Where *is she?* _____

Those aren't candles. What *are they?* _____

1. Tino isn't here. Where _____

2. This isn't Coca-cola. What _____

3. That woman isn't Mrs. Golo. Who _____

4. The magazines aren't in the living room? Where _____

5. Those aren't vases. What _____

6. Those people aren't the Browns. Who _____

7. Maria isn't at home. Where _____

8. This isn't aspirin. What _____

9. That man isn't Mr. Bascomb. Who _____

10. Those aren't post cards. What _____

11. The letters aren't in the desk. Where _____

12. That girl isn't Linda. Who _____

38

d *Write sentences about the pictures on the right side of the page.*

This man is strong.

1. *That man is weak.*

This woman is happy.

2. _____

This car is new.

3. _____

This man is hot.

4. _____

This cat is white.

5. _____

e *Write sentences about the pictures on the right side of the page.*

These men are rich.

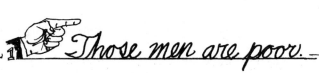

1. *Those men are poor.*

These women are fat.

2. _____

These windows are open.

3. _____

These shoes are cheap.

4. _____

These women are old.

5. _____

SUBJECT AND OBJECT PRONOUNS

he — him	we — us
she — her	they — them
I — me	it — it

f *Complete the following sentences using subject pronouns and object pronouns.*

Examples: Miss Hackey isn't a secretary. __*She*__ 's a movie star.

She's a beautiful woman. Look at __*her*__.

1. Please wait for me. _____ 'm not ready.

2. That's my book. Don't take _____ .

3. Where are the girls? Are _____ at school?

4. That man isn't Mr. Smith. Who is _____ ?

5. Anne is in the hospital. Take _____ these flowers.

6. Bring Albert and me a bottle of Coca-cola. _____ 're thirsty.

7. The dishes are dirty. Please wash _____ .

8. Look outside. _____ 's a beautiful day.

9. I'm your friend. Listen to _____ .

10. Linda isn't here. Where is _____ ?

11. Peter and I are busy. Don't talk to _____ now.

12. Mr. Bascomb is at a business meeting. Please give _____ this message.

g *Change from singular to plural.*

1. man __*men*__
2. wife __*wives*__
3. city __*cities*__
4. church _____
5. flower _____
6. child _____
7. library _____
8. bus _____
9. tree _____
10. book _____
11. shelf _____
12. dictionary _____
13. watch _____
14. day _____
15. life _____
16. woman _____
17. secretary _____
18. dress _____

h *Write questions and answers about the pictures, as indicated.*

1. Pierre Dupont/45/France/painter

Who's that man?   *He's Pierre Dupont.*
How old is he?   *He's forty-five.*
Where's he from?   *He's from France.*
What's his job?   *He's a painter.*

2. Hiroko Sato/22/Japan/model

Who's that woman?   *She's Hiroko Sato.*
How old is she?   *She's twenty-two.*
Where's she from?   *She's from Japan.*
What's her job?   *She's a model.*

3. Anna Pappas/39/Greece/taxi driver

Who's _____ ? _____
How old _____ ? _____
Where's _____ ? _____
What's _____ ? _____

4. Mario Fellini/34/Italy/mechanic

Who's _____ ? _____
How old _____ ? _____
Where's _____ ? _____
What's _____ ? _____

5. Tarik Aziz/51/Egypt/engineer

man?

_he?_

from?

job?

6. Sonia Amado/26/Brazil/dancer

woman?

she?

from?

job?

7. Natasha Romanov/47/Russia/teacher

? _Natasha Romanov._

? _forty-seven._

? _Russia._

? _teacher._

8. Robert Blake/40/England/policeman

? _Robert Blake._

? _forty._

? _England._

? _policeman._

i *Ask and answer questions about the picture using these prepositions:* **in, on, next to, in front of, behind, under, between.**

Example: girl/horse *Where is the girl? She's behind the horse.*

1. boy/bicycle _____

2. man and woman/bridge _____

3. dog/bridge _____

4. Indian/cowboys _____

5. motorcycle/tree _____

6. cow/car _____

7. men/hot-air balloon _____

j *What time is it?*

1.

It's twenty minutes to nine.

2.

_____

3.

_____

4.

_____
_____

5.

_____
_____

6.

_____
_____

7.

_____
_____

8.

_____
_____

9.

_____
_____

10.

_____
_____

11.

_____
_____

12.

_____
_____

CHAPTER FIVE

Present continuous

Wh- questions

PRESENT CONTINUOUS   Affirmative

He She It	's (is)	
I	'm (am)	walking to the park.
We You They	're (are)	

give	giving	leave	leaving
take	taking	write	writing
come	coming	dance	dancing

When a verb ends in a single *e*, omit the *e* before you add *ing*.

a *Write a sentence for each picture using the present continuous.*

1. *She's buying a motorcycle.*

2. *They're going to the beach.*

3. _____

4. _____

5. _____

6. _____

48

7. ←_____

8. _____→

9. ←_____

10. _____→

11. ←_____

12. _____→

13. ←_____

14. _____→

PRESENT CONTINUOUS   Negative

He She It	isn't (is not)	walking to the park.
I	'm not (am not)	
We You They	aren't (are not)	

b *Make negative sentences.*

Examples: We're going to the post office.   (to the bank)

We aren't going to the bank.

She's opening the door.   (the window)

She isn't opening the window.

1. He's drinking coffee.   (tea)

_____

2. I'm writing a letter to Anne.   (to Barbara)

_____

3. You're listening to him.   (me)

_____

4. We're waiting for a taxi.   (the bus)

_____

5. She's watching television.   (the children)

_____

6. They're eating breakfast.   (lunch)

_____

7. He's cleaning the bedroom.   (the bathroom)

_____

8. I'm calling the hospital.   (the library)

_____

9. They're going to the movies.   (to the museum)

_____

50

PRESENT CONTINUOUS   Interrogative

Is	he she it	
Am	I	walking to the park?
Are	you we they	

c *Change to the interrogative.*

Examples: Maria is sitting with Peter.

Is Maria sitting with Peter?

They're drinking coffee.

Are they drinking coffee?

1. He's reading a magazine.

_____

2. They're waiting for Johnnie.

_____

3. He's talking to Mr. Bascomb.

_____

4. They're calling Otis.

_____

5. He's listening to Anne.

_____

6. She's playing the guitar.

_____

7. Barbara and Tino are sitting in the corner.

_____

8. They're singing a French song.

_____

9. Mr. Bascomb is going home.

_____

PRESENT CONTINUOUS   Interrogative

Is	he she	
Am	I	walking to the park?
Are	you we they	

Short Answers

	he she	is.
Yes,	I	am.
	you we they	are.

	he she	isn't.
No,	I	'm not.
	you we they	aren't.

d *Look at the pictures and answer the questions.*

1. Is Jimmy listening to records?

   Yes, he is.

2. Is Johnnie listening to records?

   No, he isn't. He's watching television.

3. Are Albert and Linda waiting for a taxi?

   _____

4. Are Mr. and Mrs. Bascomb playing the piano?

   _____

5. Is Albert eating an apple?

_____

6. Are Jimmy and Linda washing the dishes?

_____

7. Is Mrs. Golo reading a book?

_____

8. Are Peter and Maria going to the museum?

_____

9. Is Mr. Bascomb buying a vase?

_____

Question with WHERE, WHAT, WHO

Where's	the teacher?
Where are	the students?
What's	he doing?
What are	they doing?
Who's	he talking to?
Who are	they talking to?

e *Write questions using **where**, **what**, or **who**.*

Examples: Mr. Bascomb is in the kitchen.

Where's Mr. Bascomb?

He's reading the newspaper.

What's he reading?

1. Mrs. Golo is at home.

_____

2. She's looking at the telephone book.

_____

3. She's calling Mrs. Brown.

_____

4. Gloria is with Otis.

_____

5. They're at the market.

_____

6. They're buying fruit and vegetables.

_____

7. Albert is standing at the bus stop.

_____

8. He's talking to Linda.

_____

9. They're waiting for the bus.

_____

SUBJECT AND OBJECT PRONOUNS

I — me	we — us
you — you	they — them
he — him	it — it
she — her	

f *Answer the following questions using object pronouns.*

Examples: What's Barbara giving <u>Tino</u>? (a watch)

She's giving him a watch.

How much is Mr. Bascomb paying <u>his secretaries</u>? ($5.00 an hour)

He's paying them five dollars an hour.

1. What's Albert taking <u>Linda</u>? (a letter)

_____

2. What's Otis giving <u>his friends</u>? (a bag of apples)

_____

3. What's Mrs. Golo bringing <u>you and me</u>? (a cat)

_____

4. How much is Barney giving <u>the waiter</u>? ($10.00)

_____

5. What's Peter <u>taking Maria</u>? (a vase)

_____

6. What's Nancy bringing <u>you and me</u>? (a lamp)

_____

7. What's Mrs. Brown taking <u>the Golos</u>? (a record player)

_____

8. What's Otis buying <u>Gloria</u>? (a hat)

_____

9. What's Anne bringing <u>Mr. Bascomb</u>? (a dictionary)

_____

CHAPTER SIX

"To have"   Possessive of nouns
Possessive   "Whose . . .?"
adjectives

TO HAVE   Affirmative

He She	has	
I You We They	have	a car.

a *Write a sentence for each picture using the verb to have.*

1. *She has a handbag.*

2. *They have a refrigerator.*

3. _____

4. _____

5. _____

6. _____

58

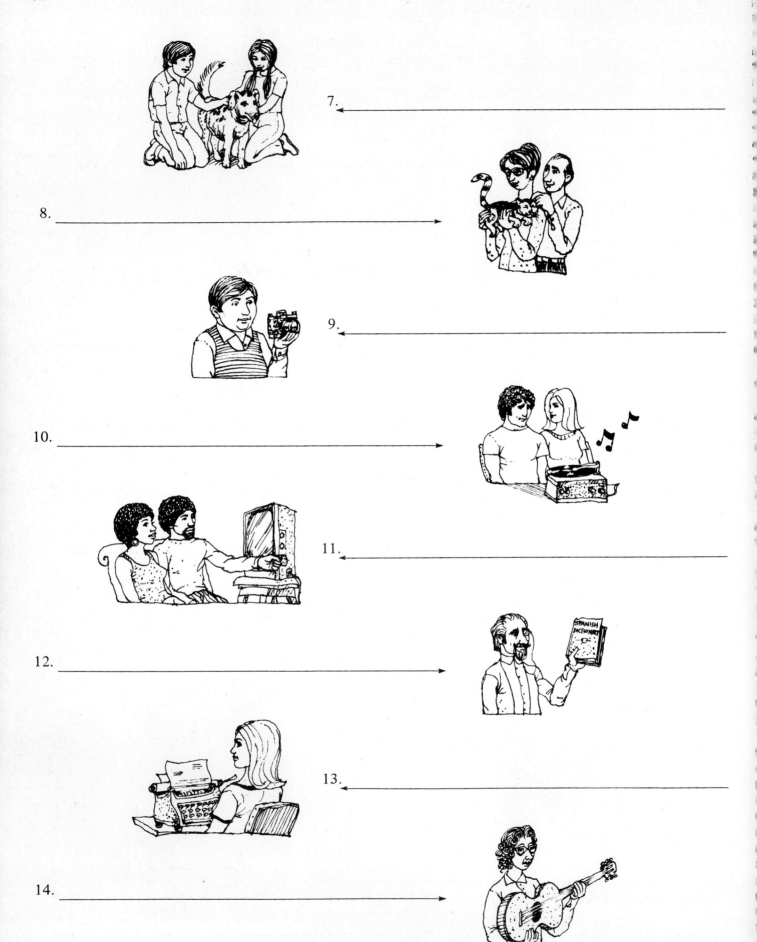

7.

8.

9.

10.

11.

12.

13.

14.

TO HAVE   Negative

He She	doesn't (does not)	
I You We They	don't (do not)	have a car.

b *Make negative sentences:*

Examples: She has a clock.   (a watch)

But she doesn't have a watch.

They have a radio.   (a television)

But they don't have a television.

1. You have a coat.   (a hat)

_____

2. I have a table.   (a desk)

_____

3. He has a French dictionary.   (a Spanish dictionary)

_____

4. She has a guitar.   (a piano)

_____

5. We have your lamp.   (your vase)

_____

6. I have your telephone number.   (your address)

_____

7. He has a cat.   (a dog)

_____

8. She has a job.   (a car)

_____

9. They have an office.   (a telephone)

_____

60

TO HAVE   Interrogative

Does	he she	
Do	I you we they	have a car?

c *Change to the interrogative.*

Examples: He has a watch.

Does he have a watch?

You have a telephone.

Do you have a television?

1. They have a stove.

_____

2. She has a brown handbag.

_____

3. I have your telephone number.

_____

4. He has an Italian car.

_____

5. We have a large vase.

_____

6. She has a guitar.

_____

7. They have a record player.

_____

8. You have a dog.

_____

9. He has an apple.

_____

TO HAVE   Interrogative

Does	he she	have a car?
Do	I you we they	

Short Answers

Yes,	he she	does.
	I you we they	do.

No,	he she	doesn't.
	I you we they	don't.

d *Look at the pictures and answer the questions.*

1. Do Sam and Mabel have a garden?

   Yes, they do.

2. Do Jimmy and Linda have a cat?

   No, they don't. They have a dog.

3. Does Nancy have a motorcycle?

   _____

4. Does Albert have an apple?

   _____

5. Does Barney have a truck?

_____

6. Do Mr. and Mrs. Golo have a refrigerator?

_____

7. Does Simon have a rabbit?

_____

8. Does Mr. Poole have a hat?

_____

9. Do Barbara and Tino have a motorcycle?

_____

POSSESSIVE ADJECTIVES

I	— my	she	— her
you	— your	we	— our
he	— his	they	— their

e *Write sentences using the possessive adjective.*

Examples: I have a typewriter. *It's my typewriter.*

She has a handbag. *It's her handbag.*

1. They have a camera. _____

2. He has a motorcycle. _____

3. You have a guitar. _____

4. She has a dictionary. _____

5. I have a clock. _____

6. We have a refrigerator. _____

7. He has a coat. _____

8. I have a lamp. _____

f *Change the following sentences using the possessive adjective.*

Examples: He has a beautiful sister. *His sister is beautiful.*

They have an old car. *Their car is old.*

1. She has an intelligent boyfriend. _____

2. They have a French doctor. _____

3. We have a new television. _____

4. He has a black umbrella. _____

5. I have a hungry dog. _____

6. They have a Japanese camera. _____

7. You have a beautiful garden. _____

8. She has a young mother. _____

64

Question with WHOSE	
Whose	glasses are those?
	football is this?

POSSESSIVE OF NOUNS
They're Mabel's glasses.
It's the boys' football.

g *Answer the following questions as indicated.*

Examples: Whose cards are those? (Tino) *They're Tino's cards.*

Whose cat is that? (the Golos) *It's the Golos' cat.*

1. Whose chickens are those? (Simon) _____

2. Whose garden is that? (the Browns) _____

3. Whose flowers are those? (Barbara) _____

4. Whose vase is that? (Mrs. Brown) _____

5. Whose letter is this? (Albert) _____

6. Whose magazines are these? (the girls) _____

7. Whose envelopes are those? (Mr. Grubb) _____

8. Whose pencil is this? (Linda) _____

h *Make questions with* **whose.**

Examples: Look at those cats! *Whose cats are they?*

Look at that dog! *Whose dog is it?*

1. Look at that camera! _____

2. Look at this typewriter! _____

3. Look at those hats! _____

4. Look at those flowers! _____

5. Look at that house! _____

6. Look at this guitar! _____

7. Look at those bicycles! _____

8. Look at that car! _____

CHAPTER SEVEN

"There is"/
"there are"
Uncountables

"To want" and
"to like"
Possessive
pronouns

a *Look at the picture and answer the questions using **there's a**.*

Examples: What's in the left corner? (clock) *There's a clock in the left corner.*

What's behind the couch? (wastebasket) *There's a wastebasket behind the couch.*

1. What's in front of the couch? (table) _____

2. What's under the table? (telephone) _____

3. What's in front of the desk? (chair) _____

4. What's on the desk? (typewriter) _____

5. What's next to the typewriter? (lamp) _____

6. What's in the right corner? (television) _____

7. What's on the wall? (mirror) _____

68

b *Look at the picture and write sentences using **there are some**.*

Example: cups/shelf *There are some cups on the shelf.*

1. candles/table _____

2. books/chair _____

3. magazines/floor _____

4. oranges/table _____

5. glasses/shelf _____

6. pots/wall _____

7. flowers/vase _____

8. dishes/shelf _____

c *Answer the following questions using **there's a** or **it's a**.*

Examples: What's on the shelf? (a dictionary) *There's a dictionary on the shelf.*

What kind of dictionary is it? (Japanese) *It's a Japanese dictionary.*

1. What's in the closet? (a guitar) _____

What kind of guitar is it? (Spanish) _____

2. What's on the desk? (a typewriter) _____

What kind of typewriter is it? (electric) _____

3. What's in the back yard? (a garden) _____

What kind of garden is it? (vegetable) _____

4. What's on the table? (a bowl) _____

What kind of bowl is it? (soup) _____

d *Answer the following questions using **there are some** or **they're**.*

Examples: What's in the closet? (shoes) *There are some shoes in the closet.*

What kind of shoes are they? (tennis) *They're tennis shoes.*

1. What's on the shelf? (cups) _____

What kind of cups are they? (paper) _____

2. What's on the table? (records) _____

What kind of records are they? (jazz) _____

3. What's in the handbag? (cigarettes) _____

What kind of cigarettes are they? (French) _____

4. What's in the desk? (letters) _____

What kind of letters are they? (business) _____

70

e *Write a sentence for each picture using **there's some**.*

1. cereal/box

There's some cereal in the box.

2. ice cream/carton

_____

3. soup/can

_____

4. orange juice/bottle

_____

5. tea/teapot

_____

6. sugar/bowl

_____

7. honey/jar

_____

8. flour/bag

_____

f *Write sentences about the objects in the picture using* **there's a**, **there's some**, *or* **there are some**.

Examples: bowl/table *There's a bowl on the table.*

soup/bowl *There's some soup in the bowl.*

bananas/table *There are some bananas on the table.*

1. dish/table _____

2. ice cream/dish _____

3. sandwiches/table _____

4. bottle/table _____

5. orange juice/bottle _____

6. box/table _____

7. apples/box _____

72

g *List the following words according to the underlined vowel sound.*

make	candle	take	ask	game	mechanic
class	paper	camera	salesman	taxi	airplane
family	name	handbag	apple	gas	nationality
table	happy	radio	dangerous	station	lemonade

vase (ey)   **lamp (ae)**

make _____   _____   *class* _____   _____

_____   _____   _____   _____

_____   _____   _____   _____

_____   _____   _____   _____

_____   _____   _____   _____

fine	price	tonight	write	wife
bring	sister	give	window	dish
big	bicycle	life	single	kitchen
behind	drive	nice	right	light
city	capital	office	dinner	

time (ay)   **think (i)**

fine _____   _____   *bring* _____   _____

_____   _____   _____   _____

_____   _____   _____   _____

_____   _____   _____   _____

_____   _____   _____   _____

h *Write a sentence for each picture using the verb* **to like.**

1. *They like classical music.*

2. *He likes butterflies.*

3. _____

4. _____

5. _____

6. _____

7. _____

8. _____

74

*i Write a sentence for each picture using the verb **to want**.*

1. _She wants a handbag._

2. _They want a clock._

3. _____

4. _____

5. _____

6. _____

7. _____

8. _____

POSSESSIVE PRONOUNS

my — mine	her — hers
your — yours	our — ours
his — his	their — theirs

j *Write sentences using the possessive pronoun.*

Examples: That house belongs to Dr. Pasto. *It's his.* _____

This vase belongs to me. *It's mine.* _____

1. That table belongs to Anne. _____

2. This record player belongs to Jimmy and Linda. _____

3. That chair belongs to Tino. _____

4. This typewriter belongs to us. _____

5. That handbag belongs to Maria. _____

6. This pen belongs to you. _____

7. This watch belongs to him. _____

8. That dog belongs to me. _____

k *Change the following sentences using the possessive pronoun.*

Examples: This is your pen. *This pen is yours.* _____

That's her coat. *That coat is hers.* _____

1. That's our clock. _____

2. This is my dictionary. _____

3. This is her newspaper. _____

4. That's your umbrella. _____

5. This is my guitar. _____

6. That's their lamp. _____

7. This is our book. _____

8. That's his motorcycle. _____

Complete the dialogue.

SAM: This closet's a mess.

MABEL: It certainly is.

SAM: Whose umbrella _____?

MABEL: It's Linda's.

SAM: _____ hat _____?

MABEL: It's Jimmy's.

SAM: _____ magazines _____?

MABEL: _____.

SAM: _____ shoes _____?

MABEL: _____, Sam.

CHAPTER EIGHT

Review

a *Write sentences about the objects in the picture using the prepositions **in**, **on**, **next to**, **in front of**, **behind**,*
*or **under**.*

Example: newspaper/bed *There's a newspaper on the bed.* _____

1. dog/bed _____

2. shoe/dog _____

3. lamp/table _____

4. clock/lamp _____

5. coat/closet _____

6. cat/door _____

7. picture/wall _____

80

PLURALS

box	boxes	city	cities
glass	glasses	library	libraries
peach	peaches	secretary	secretaries

Irregular Plurals

man	men
woman	women
child	children

b *Change from singular to plural.*

Examples: There's a picture on the wall.

There are some pictures on the wall.

There's an old woman at the bus stop.

There are some old women at the bus stop.

1. There's a dog in the restaurant.

_____

2. There's a man in front of the bank.

_____

3. There's a dictionary in the office.

_____

4. There's a magazine next to the typewriter.

_____

5. There's a flower in the vase.

_____

6. There's a dish on the shelf.

_____

7. There's a bicycle behind the house.

_____

8. There's a bus in the street.

_____

9. There's a bird in the tree.

_____

10. There's a candle by the window.

_____

c *Look at the pictures and answer the questions.*

1. Are Barbara and Tino playing cards?

Yes, they are.

2. Is Otis playing cards?

No, he isn't. He's playing chess.

3. Is Peter taking a shower?

_____

4. Are Peter and Maria sitting in a restaurant?

_____

5. Are they looking at the clock?

_____

6. Is Mrs. Golo calling the hospital?

_____

7. Are Barbara and Tino talking to Dr. Pasto?

_____

8. Are they paying the waiter?

_____

9. Is Robert opening the window?

_____

10. Are Albert and Linda waiting for the bus?

_____

d *Complete the following sentences with suitable prepositions.*

Example: Sam's working ___*in*___ the garden ___*with*___ Mabel.

1. Sam is thirsty. He's going _____ the kitchen _____ a glass _____ water.

2. He's taking a glass _____ the shelf.

3. Is there any ice _____ the refrigerator?

4. Jimmy is playing cards _____ Linda.

5. They're sitting _____ the floor _____ the living room.

6. Nick is working _____ the garage _____ Maple Street.

7. Otis is buying some flowers _____ Gloria.

8. Maria is going _____ the park _____ Peter.

9. They're talking _____ music.

e *Change the following sentences to the plural.*

Examples: This is a good sandwich. *These are good sandwiches.* _____

That's a small orange. *Those are small oranges.* _____

1. This is an expensive pen. _____

2. That's a beautiful vase. _____

3. That's an interesting picture. _____

4. This is a good dictionary. _____

5. That's a Japanese camera. _____

6. This is a new record. _____

7. This is a large envelope. _____

8. That's an interesting magazine. _____

9. This is an old book. _____

84

f *Write sentences as indicated.*

Examples: Albert/lemonade *Albert likes lemonade, but he doesn't want any right now.*

Jimmy and Linda/ice cream *Jimmy and Linda like ice cream, but they don't want any right now.*

1. Anne/orange juice _____

2. I/Coca-cola _____

3. Mr. Bascomb/coffee _____

4. The Golos/tea _____

5. Maria/apple juice _____

6. We/tomato soup _____

7. Peter/French fries _____

8. Miss Hackey/milk _____

9. Barbara and Tino/chocolates _____

_____

g *Answer the following questions about yourself.*

1. Where are you now? _____

2. What are you wearing? _____

3. What color are your shoes? _____

4. Do you have a record player? _____

5. Do you like rock'n'roll? _____

6. What kind of movies do you like? _____

7. What do you want for your birthday? _____

8. What do you have in your wallet/handbag? _____

9. What country are you from? _____

10. How many people are there in your family? _____

11. How many brothers and sisters do you have? _____

12. Are you happy or sad today? _____

h *Look at the pictures and complete the following sentences as indicated.*

i *Write a short composition about the picture.*
*Use the present continuous, **there is**, and*
***there are**.*

policeman	Mr. Bascomb	chase	taxi	window	at the corner
firemen	Barney	eat	fire truck	roof	in the street
children		open	snack bar	dogs	on the roof
tourists	stand	leave	pet shop	cat	
old woman	look at	smoke	theater	birds	
young woman	drive		drugstore	cigar	
				hot dogs	

88

j *Write questions and answers about the pictures, as indicated.*

bananas
☆ 29¢/lb.

1. How much are the bananas?
They're twenty-nine cents a pound.

apples
✳ 79¢/lb.

oranges
49¢/lb.

2. _____

_____

cherries
• 99¢/lb. •

3. _____

_____

Peaches
★ 69¢/lb. ★

4. _____

_____

5. _____

_____

Lemons
39¢/lb.

grapes
89¢/lb.

6. _____

_____

7. _____

_____

Pineapples
• 59¢/lb. •

8. _____

_____

CHAPTER NINE

**Present simple   Adverbs of
frequency**

PRESENT SIMPLE Affirmative

He / She	lives	in New York.
I / You / We / They	live	

a *Write a sentence for each picture using the present simple with* **every day**.

1. *She takes the bus every day.*

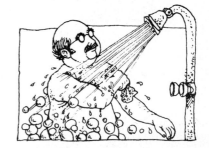

2. *They work at the bank every day.*

3. _____

4. _____

5. _____

6. _____

92

7. <--_____

8. _____-->

9. <--_____

10. _____-->

11. <--_____

12. _____-->

13. <--_____

14. _____-->

PRESENT SIMPLE   Negative

He She	doesn't	live in New York.
I You We They	don't	

b *Make negative sentences as indicated.*

Examples: We know Mr. Poole.   (his wife)

But we don't know his wife.

He plays the piano.   (the guitar)

But he doesn't play the guitar.

1. I have a dictionary.   (an encyclopedia)

_____

2. She listens to her father.   (her mother)

_____

3. They study at the library.   (at home)

_____

4. You like classical music.   (rock music)

_____

5. He writes to his friends.   (to his family)

_____

6. They work on Saturday.   (on Sunday)

_____

7. She takes the bus to school.   (the bus home)

_____

8. We know your brother.   (your sister)

_____

9. I like football.   (basketball)

_____

94

PRESENT SIMPLE   Interrogative

Does	he she	
Do	I you we they	live in New York?

c *Change to the interrogative.*

Examples: She works at the hospital.

Does she work at the hospital?

They drink coffee with milk.

Do they drink coffee with milk?

1. You walk to work.

_____

2. He listens to the radio.

_____

3. We have your telephone number.

_____

4. They play football in the park.

_____

5. She likes flowers.

_____

6. I write interesting letters.

_____

7. They come from Mexico.

_____

8. He wants a motorcycle.

_____

9. You read the newspaper.

_____

PRESENT SIMPLE   Interrogative

Does	he she	
Do	I you we they	live in New York?

Short Answers

Yes,	he she	does.
	I you we they	do.

No,	he she	doesn't.
	I you we they	don't.

d *Look at the pictures and answer the questions.*

1. Does Sam wear a white hat?

   Yes, he does. _____

2. Do the Golos live on Lime Street?

   No, they don't. They live on Maple Street.

3. Does Barney drive a bus?

   _____

4. Do Sam and Mabel work in the garden?

   _____

96

5. Do Anne and Barbara work at the post office?

_____

6. Does Maria want a hat?

_____

7. Do Mr. and Mrs. Golo like cats?

_____

8. Does Jack like cats?

_____

9. Do Jimmy and Linda want a record player?

_____

ADVERBS OF FREQUENCY

They	always usually often sometimes seldom never	take the bus.

e *Add* **always, usually, often, sometimes, seldom,** *or* **never** *to the following sentences.*

Examples: Sam wears a white hat. (always)

Sam always wears a white hat.

Nancy reads the newspaper. (sometimes)

Nancy sometimes reads the newspaper.

1. Jimmy plays football in the park. (always)

_____

2. Mr. and Mrs. Bascomb work in the garden. (never)

_____

3. Peter drinks coffee with milk. (usually)

_____

4. Anne eats at the Martinoli Restaurant. (seldom)

_____

5. Johnnie goes to the movies. (often)

_____

6. Barbara and Tino listen to classical music. (sometimes)

_____

7. Maria writes long letters. (seldom)

_____

8. Mr. Golo washes the dishes. (often)

_____

9. Dr. Pasto has lunch at one o'clock. (usually)

_____

98

f *Answer the following questions using adverbs of frequency.*

Examples: Do you watch television?

Yes, I often watch television.

OR *No, I seldom watch television.*

Do you wear a hat?

Yes, I always wear a hat.

OR *No, I never wear a hat.*

1. Do you eat breakfast in the morning?

_____

2. Do you drink coffee?

_____

3. Do you go to the park?

_____

4. Do you play tennis?

_____

5. Do you study in the library?

_____

6. Do you listen to your friends?

_____

7. Do you talk about sports?

_____

8. Do you dance at parties?

_____

9. Do you sing in the shower?

_____

10. Do you play cards?

_____

CHAPTER TEN

Present simple vs. present continuous

Other/another
Some/any

PRESENT CONTINUOUS

He's	reading the newspaper. drinking coffee. listening to the radio. wearing a white hat.

PRESENT SIMPLE

He	reads the newspaper drinks coffee listens to the radio wears a white hat	every day.

a *Rewrite the following sentences using the present simple with **every day**.*

Example: Barney is driving his taxi.

Barney drives his taxi every day.

1. Susie is writing to her boyfriend.

   _____

2. She's listening to the radio.

   _____

3. Otis is going to the park.

   _____

4. He's eating an apple.

   _____

5. Barbara is working at the bank.

   _____

6. She's talking to Anne.

   _____

7. Sam is walking home.

   _____

8. He's wearing his white hat.

   _____

9. Linda is studying in the library.

   _____

10. She's waiting for Albert.

   _____

PRESENT SIMPLE

She often	talks on the phone. watches television. writes letters. wears a red dress.

PRESENT CONTINUOUS

Is she	talking on the phone watching television writing a letter wearing a red dress	now?

b *Make questions using the present continuous.*

Example: Linda usually helps her friends.

Is she helping her friends now?

1. Nancy often reads a book.

_____

2. She sometimes goes to the movies.

_____

3. Mr. Bascomb usually drinks coffee.

_____

4. He seldom washes the dishes.

_____

5. Mabel sometimes calls Mrs. Golo.

_____

6. They often talk about their husbands.

_____

7. Dr. Pasto usually listens to classical music.

_____

8. He seldom plays the piano.

_____

9. Tino often walks home.

_____

10. He seldom looks at his watch.

_____

SOME/ANY   Affirmative

She has They have	some	apples. oranges. bread. butter.

c *Write an affirmative sentence for each picture using the verb* **to have** *with* **some.**

1. *He has some cigarettes.*

2. *They have some magazines.*

3. _____

4. _____

5. _____

6. _____

7. _____

8. _____

104

SOME/ANY   Negative

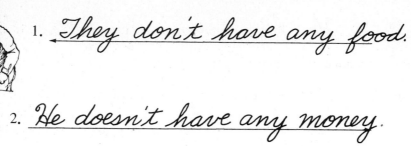

She doesn't have	any	apples. oranges. bread. butter.
They don't have		

d *Write a negative sentence for each picture using the verb* **to have** *with* **any**.

1. *They don't have any food.*

2. *He doesn't have any money.*

3. _____

4. _____

5. _____

6. _____

7. _____

8. _____

SOME/ANY   Interrogative

Does she have		apples?
	any	oranges?
Do they have		bread?
		butter?

Are there		apples?
	any	oranges?
Is there		bread?
		butter?

e *Change to the interrogative.*

Examples: There are some apples in the bag.

Are there any apples in the bag?

Barbara has some chocolates.

Does Barbara have any chocolates?

1. There's some orange juice in the refrigerator.

_____

2. There's some soup in the bowl.

_____

3. There are some magazines in the living room.

_____

4. You have some interesting books.

_____

5. He has some English records.

_____

6. They have some letters from France.

_____

7. There are some envelopes in the desk.

_____

8. There's some paper on the table.

_____

9. There are some stamps in the desk.

_____

106

f *Make sentences using **one** and **the other**.*

Examples: There are two hats in the closet. (yours/mine)

One is yours and the other is mine.

There are two candles in the box. (white/yellow)

One is white and the other is yellow.

1. There are two bottles on the shelf. (large/small)

_____

2. There are two clocks in the living room. (old/new)

_____

3. There are two cameras in the bedroom. (American/Japanese)

_____

4. There are two typewriters in the office. (cheap/expensive)

_____

5. There are two telegrams on the desk. (from Paris/from Tokyo)

_____

6. There are two newspapers in Wickam City. (good/bad)

_____

7. There are two markets on Main Street. (next to the bank/next to the library)

_____

8. There are two boys on the corner. (tall/short)

_____

9. There are two bicycles under the tree. (red/green)

_____

10. There are two cars in the street. (clean/dirty)

_____

g *Write a short composition about the picture. Use the present continuous and the present simple.*

old woman	Barney	eat	like	flowers	cup of coffee
Mr. Bascomb	Mrs. Golo	open	have	newspaper	restaurant
Tino		hold	go	motorcycle	library
Peter and Maria	sit	sing	listen to	bottle	taxi
Dr. Pasto	stand	play			
Anne and Nancy	talk	read	each other		
young man	buy		spaghetti		

108

h *List the following words in the blanks below according to the underlined vowel sounds.*

tree speak desk breakfast she French
clean next weak coffee secretary movies
dress museum ready read envelope meet
bread expensive cheap letter these hello

bed (e)   **street (iy)**

dress   *tree*

i *List the following verbs in the blanks below according to their s endings.*

gives helps lives drinks crosses loses
wants takes watches leaves writes paints
sings brushes kisses closes plays washes
dances forgets eats calls wins cleans

likes (s)   **buys (z)**   **watches (iz)**

wants   *gives*   *dances*

CHAPTER ELEVEN

"To need"
Can

Some/any/one as
pronouns

NEED Affirmative

He	needs	a pencil.
They	need	some paper.

a *Write a sentence for each picture using the verb* **to need**.

1. *They need some socks.*

2. *He needs a secretary.*

3. _____

4. _____

5. _____

6. _____

112

7. ⟵_____

8. _____⟶

9. ⟵_____

10. _____⟶

11. ⟵_____

12. _____⟶

13. ⟵_____

14. _____⟶

b *Look at the pictures and answer the questions.*

1. Does Barney need socks?

   Yes, he does.

2. Does Mrs. Bascomb need bread?

   No, she doesn't. She needs butter.

3. Do Jimmy and Linda need jam?

   _____

4. Do those men need money?

   _____

5. Does that man need a hat?

   _____

114

6. Does Maria need sugar?

_____

7. Does Peter need cigarettes?

_____

8. Do Otis and Gloria need envelopes?

_____

9. Do Mr. and Mrs. Bascomb need food?

_____

10. Does Barney need oil?

_____

CAN	Affirmative	
He She I You We They	can	swim.

c *Write a sentence for each picture using the verb* ***can.***

1. play basketball *He can play basketball.*

2. ski _____

3. dance ⟵_____

4. cook _____⟶

5. swim ⟵_____

6. play the piano _____⟶

7. sing ⟵_____

8. write poetry _____⟶

116

CAN Negative

He She I You We They	can't (cannot)	swim.

CAN Interrogative

Can	he she I you we they	ski?

d *Make questions as indicated.*

Example: He can't speak German. (Italian)

Can he speak Italian?

1. They can't play chess. (checkers)

_____

2. She can't ride a motorcycle. (a bicycle)

_____

3. He can't drive a truck. (a bus)

_____

4. We can't buy a television. (a radio)

_____

5. They can't speak Portuguese. (Spanish)

_____

6. She can't draw animals. (people)

_____

7. She can't play the violin. (the guitar)

_____

8. He can't sing. (dance)

_____

9. He can't do the samba. (the tango)

_____

e *Complete the following sentences using the phrases below. Use each phrase only once.*

up the tree	in the river	through the gate
out of the water	from the tree	under the bridge
by the fire	over the fence	
across the bridge	after the cat	

Example: The truck is passing ___*through the gate.*___

1. The man is fishing _____

2. The fish are jumping _____

3. The horse is jumping _____

4. The girl is walking _____

5. The young couple is standing _____

6. The boy is climbing _____

7. The leaves are falling _____

8. The bum is sitting _____

9. The dog is running _____

CHAPTER TWELVE

Review

a *Answer the following questions as indicated.*

1. Pierre Dupont/Paris/French

   Where does Pierre Dupont live?

   He lives in Paris.

   What language does he speak?

   He speaks French.

2. Hiroko Sato/Tokyo/Japanese

   Where does Hiroko Sato live?

   _____

   What language does she speak?

   _____

3. Anna Pappas/Athens/Greek

   Where does Anna Pappas live?

   _____

   What language does she speak?

   _____

4. Mario Fellini/Rome/Italian

   Where does Mario Fellini live?

   _____

   What language does he speak?

   _____

122

5. Tarik Aziz/Cairo/Arabic

Where does Tarik Aziz live?

_____

What language does he speak?

_____

6. Sonia Amado/Rio de Janeiro/Portuguese

Where does Sonia Amado live?

_____

What language does she speak?

_____

7. Natasha Romanov/Moscow/Russian

Where does Natasha Romanov live?

_____

What language does she speak?

_____

8. Robert Blake/London/English

Where does Robert Blake live?

_____

What language does he speak?

_____

b *Write affirmative commands after the following sentences, using the verbs from the list below. Use each verb only once.*

help	wash	drink	pay
listen to	take	read	answer
feed	look at	close	

Examples: Barbara is beautiful tonight. *Look at her.*

The dogs are hungry. *Feed them.*

1. Your hands are dirty. _____

2. The phone is ringing. _____

3. This coffee is delicious. _____

4. The waiter is coming with the bill. _____

5. The car door is open. _____

6. Here are your keys. _____

7. What does the letter say? _____

8. She can't do it without you. _____

9. The birds are singing. _____

c *Write negative commands after the following sentences, using the verbs from the list below. Use each verb only once.*

drive	close	bother	leave
wear	cut	drink	eat
use	read	buy	

Examples: The typewriter is broken. *Don't use it.*

I'm very busy. *Don't bother me.*

a broken typewriter

1. That letter isn't yours. _____

2. I can't live without you. _____

3. That car is dangerous. _____

4. Leave the window open. _____

5. That coffee is terrible. _____

6. Those pants aren't clean. _____

7. I like your hair long. _____

8. Those shoes are very expensive. _____

9. Hey, that's my sandwich. _____

124

d *Write a sentence about each picture using* **can't**.

1. *She can't get in the car.*

2. _____

3. _____

4. _____

5. _____

6. _____

We're out of detergent!

7. _____

8. _____

e *Make questions using* **who, what,** *or* **where**.

Examples: Jimmy's <u>at home</u>. *Where is he?*

He's with <u>his sister</u>. *Who is he with?*

They're looking at <u>photographs</u>. *What are they looking at?*

1. Gloria is with <u>her boyfriend</u>. _____

2. They're <u>at the bus stop</u>. _____

3. They're wearing <u>jeans</u>. _____

4. Mr. and Mrs. Bascomb are <u>in the living room</u>. _____

5. They're talking with <u>Dr. Pasto</u>. _____

6. They're listening to <u>classical music</u>. _____

7. Tino is <u>in his car</u>. _____

8. He's eating <u>an apple</u>. _____

9. He's waiting for <u>Barbara</u>. _____

f *Write original sentences using the following words and expressions.*

Example: every day *I take the bus every day.*

1. near _____

2. because _____

3. any _____

4. now _____

5. sometimes _____

6. another _____

7. a good time _____

8. how many _____

9. what kind _____

10. about _____

11. late _____

12. expensive _____

g *Answer the following questions about the advertisement.*

1. When does the sale start? *It starts today at ten a.m.*

2. How long does the sale last? _____

3. What is the regular price of brass beds? _____

4. What is the sale price of brass beds? _____

5. How much can you save on a brass bed during the sale? _____

6. How much can you save on dining tables? _____

7. What do the first twenty customers get? _____

8. What hours is the store open on weekdays? _____

9. Is the store open on Sundays? _____

10. What's the address of Mason's Furniture Store? _____

h *Write questions and answers about the pictures, as indicated.*

1. Sam/grass/once a month

What's Sam doing?
He's cutting the grass. He cuts
the grass once a month.

2. Anne and Barbara/letters/every day

What are Anne and Barbara
doing? They're typing letters.
They type letters every day.

3. Mrs. Golo/cat/twice a day

_____

_____

4. Fred and Barney/cards/every weekend

_____

_____

_____

128

5. Maria/hair/three times a week

_____

_____

_____

6. Jimmy and Linda/homework/every night

_____

_____

_____

7. Dr. Pasto/breakfast/every morning

_____

_____

_____

8. Sam and Jack/football game/every Sunday

_____

_____

_____

i *Complete the following sentences using the prepositions* **in, on,** *and* **at.**

Examples: Mary lives *in* San Francisco.

She lives *on* Lombard Street.

She lives *at* 905 Lombard St.

> Note: in → cities, towns, countries
> on → streeets, roads, avenues
> at → street addresses

1. Johnnie Wilson lives _____ Wickam City.

2. He has a book store _____ Bond Street.

3. His apartment is _____ 182 Franklin Avenue.

4. Do you live _____ a large city?

5. How many houses are there _____ your street?

6. Do you and your sister live _____ the same address?

7. I live _____ a small town.

8. My house is _____ a wide, beautiful street.

9. I work at the Park Hotel _____ 356 Main Street.

10. My office is _____ the first floor.

11. You can call me _____ the hotel.

12. The number is _____ the telephone book.

j *Complete the following sentences.*

Example: I feel good when *I'm with my friends*.

1. I like you because _____

2. Tell me about _____

3. Where do you _____

4. I always have a good time when _____

5. How often _____

6. Some people _____

7. What time _____

8. We never _____

9. Can you _____

130

k *Answer the following questions about yourself.*

1. Where do you study?

_____

2. Do you study alone or with friends?

_____

3. Can you think when there are other people in the room?

_____

4. Do you get mad when people talk in the library?

_____

5. How much time do you need to do your homework?

_____

6. What can you learn from books?

_____

7. What time do you go to bed?

_____

8. Do you sleep with the window open or closed?

_____

9. Can you sleep with the radio on?

_____

10. How many hours (of) sleep do you need?

_____

11. Do you ever get telephone calls late at night?

_____

12. How many phone calls do you make every day?

_____

13. Who do you call?

_____

CHAPTER THIRTEEN

Simple past:	Tag questions
"to be"	Ordinal numbers

Past of TO BE   Affirmative

| I
He
She | was | |
| You
We
They | were | in Paris yesterday. |

a *Write a sentence for each picture using **was** or **were**.*

1. *They were at home yesterday.*

2. *He was at the office yesterday.*

3. _____

4. _____

5. _____

6. _____

134

7.

8.

9.

10.

11.

12.

13.

14.

Past of TO BE   Negative

I He She	wasn't (was not)	in Paris yesterday.
You We They	weren't (were not)	

b *Make negative sentences as indicated.*

Examples: It was cloudy yesterday. (sunny)

It wasn't sunny. _____

We were at the museum last Saturday. (at the library)

We weren't at the library. _____

1. I was at the bank this morning. (at the post office)

_____

2. He was at work yesterday. (at home)

_____

3. It was warm last week. (cold)

_____

4. We were at the garage yesterday afternoon. (at the market)

_____

5. You were at the park last weekend. (at the beach)

_____

6. The beach was clean last year. (dirty)

_____

7. He was a football player in high school. (a basketball player)

_____

8. She was a history student at the university. (a business student)

_____

9. They were in New York last month. (in California)

_____

136

Past of TO BE   Interrogative

Was	he she I	in Paris yesterday?
Were	you we they	

c *Change to the interrogative.*

Examples: He was your doctor last year.

Was he your doctor last year?

You were his patient.

Were you his patient?

1. They were in Bombay last month.

_____

2. You were in London.

_____

3. It was hot in India.

_____

4. It was cold in England.

_____

5. She was sick last night.

_____

6. He was sad.

_____

7. We were on Lime Street yesterday.

_____

8. I was with Nancy.

_____

9. You were at the bank.

_____

Past of TO BE   Interrogative

Was	he she I	in Paris yesterday?
Were	you we they	

Short Answers

Yes,	he she I	was.
	you we they	were.

No,	he she I	wasn't.
	you we they	weren't.

d *Look at the pictures and answer the questions.*

1. Was Mabel at home yesterday afternoon?

Yes, she was. _____

2. Was Ula at home?

No, she wasn't. She was at the movies.

3. Were Nick and Barney at the garage?

_____

4. Were Jimmy and Linda at the beach?

_____

138

5. Was Dr. Pasto at the museum?

_____

6. Was Maria at the hospital?

_____

7. Were the Golos at home?

_____

8. Were Barbara and Tino at the movies?

_____

9. Were Otis and Gloria at the market?

_____

TAG QUESTIONS

It's a beautiful day,	isn't it?
They're going to the beach,	aren't they?
You have an umbrella,	don't you?
She was at the movies,	wasn't she?
He can play the piano,	can't he?

e *Add tag questions to the following sentences.*

Examples: Jimmy is watching television.

Jimmy is watching television, isn't he?

You like football.

You like football, don't you?

1. Anne can play the guitar.

_____

2. Barney drives a taxi.

_____

3. It's hot today.

_____

4. Barbara and Tino are going to the park.

_____

5. Sam always wears a hat.

_____

6. He was at the hospital yesterday.

_____

7. You were at home last night.

_____

8. There's some bread on the table.

_____

9. We need some butter.

_____

TAG QUESTIONS

There aren't any matches,	are there?
He isn't working today,	is he?
They don't like football,	do they?
You weren't at the party,	were you?
She can't drive a truck,	can she?

f *Add tag questions to the following sentences.*

Examples: Mr. Poole doesn't like football.

Mr. Poole doesn't like football, does he?

He wasn't at the game last night.

He wasn't at the game last night, was he?

1. Mrs. Brown isn't cleaning the kitchen.

_____

2. There isn't any fruit in the refrigerator.

_____

3. The children aren't hungry.

_____

4. They weren't at the park this morning.

_____

5. Your friends aren't working today.

_____

6. They don't have a car.

_____

7. Mr. Poole doesn't like sports.

_____

8. He can't play tennis.

_____

9. It isn't raining outside.

_____

g *Give short answers to the following questions.*

Examples: It's hot in June, isn't it?

Yes, it is. OR *No, it isn't.*

You don't like sports, do you?

Yes, I do. OR *No, I don't.*

1. There are twenty-eight days in February, aren't there?

_____

2. It was cold last month, wasn't it?

_____

3. You're going to a party next week, aren't you?

_____

4. You don't play the guitar, do you?

_____

5. There isn't any milk in your house, is there?

_____

6. You didn't go to the market, did you?

_____

7. The dishes are clean, aren't they?

_____

8. You washed them, didn't you?

_____

9. You aren't hungry, are you?

_____

CHAPTER FOURTEEN

Simple past: affirmative

Simple past: negative and interrogative

SIMPLE PAST   Regular Verbs

	opened	the door.
	entered	the house.
She	washed	the dishes.
	looked	at some magazines.
	rested	on the couch.
	waited	for a telephone call.

a *Practice reading the sentences aloud. Notice the different sounds for the past endings.*

d	**t**	**id**

Mrs. Golo called the fire department.

Peter washed the car.

Otis visited the museum.

Anne played the guitar.

Sandy and Peter talked about the weather.

Dr. Pasto painted the room.

Jimmy listened to records.

Anne and Barbara worked at the bank.

Linda and Albert waited for the bus.

146

b *Write a sentence for each picture using the past tense.*

1. <u>He watched a basketball game.</u>

2. <u>They waited for the bus.</u>

3. ←_____

4. _____→

5. ←_____

6. _____→

7. ←_____

8. _____→

SIMPLE PAST   Irregular Verbs

He	bought ate took found had	some candy yesterday.

c *Practice reading the sentences aloud. Notice the irregular past forms.*

Peter drove to the beach.

Gloria made some bread.

Mr. Bascomb bought a lamp.

He took his dog.

Otis went to the park.

Anne wrote a poem.

They swam in the ocean.

Linda and Jimmy ate ice cream.

Barney found a dollar.

d *Write a sentence for each picture using the past tense.*

1. _She made a cake._

2. _____

3. _____

4. _____

5. _____

6. _____

7. _____

8. _____

SIMPLE PAST   Negative

He She I You We They	didn't (did not)	walk drive take the bus	last week.

e   *Make negative sentences as indicated.*

Example: She visited the art museum. (the music center)

She didn't visit the music center.

1. He went to the post office. (to the hospital)

_____

2. He waited for his girlfriend. (his sister)

_____

3. She arrived at two o'clock. (at three o'clock)

_____

4. They walked to the market. (to the drugstore)

_____

5. They bought fruit. (candy)

_____

6. We saw them on Lime Street. (on Main Street)

_____

7. I was hungry. (thirsty)

_____

8. They gave me an orange. (an apple)

_____

9. You ate a peach. (a pear)

_____

10. We took the bus home. (a taxi)

_____

150

SIMPLE PAST   Interrogative

Did	he she I you we they	walk drive take the bus	last week?

f *Change to the interrogative.*

Example: You had a brown hat.

Did you have a brown hat?

1. Barbara and Tino drove to the park.

_____

2. Anne went with them.

_____

3. She took her guitar.

_____

4. Barbara made some sandwiches.

_____

5. Tino brought some drinks.

_____

6. They had some ice cream for dessert.

_____

7. Anne played the guitar.

_____

8. They talked about music and art.

_____

9. Tino wrote a poem.

_____

10. Barbara painted a picture.

_____

SIMPLE PAST   Interrogative

Did	he she I you we they	walk drive take the bus	last week?

Short Answers

Yes,	he she I you we they	did.

No,	he she I you we they	didn't.

g *Look at the pictures and answer the questions.*

1. Did Mrs. Bascomb take a shower?

No, she didn't. She took a bath.

2. Did she make tea for breakfast?

Yes, she did.

3. Did Dr. Pasto paint the room?

_____

4. Did Anne and Nancy play cards?

_____

5. Did Barney find a dollar?

_____

6. Did Jimmy and Linda eat cake?

_____

7. Did Otis watch a football game?

_____

8. Did Susie write a letter?

_____

9. Did Dr. Pasto drive to the beach?

_____

h *Write a short composition about Otis and the little girl. Use the past tense.*

be	set up	like	yesterday	art equipment
go	come	give	bird	beautiful
take	look at	fly away	tree	happy
see	think	paint	picture	

154

i *List the following words according to the underlined vowel sound.*

modern	hospital	pot	hot	close	don't
office	envelope	coat	cold	shop	often
old	postcard	pocket	bottle	window	go
telephone	coffee	those	open	stop	across

home (o)

old _____   _____

clock (a)

modern _____   _____

_____   _____   _____   _____

_____   _____   _____   _____

_____   _____   _____   _____

_____   _____   _____   _____

j *List the following regular verbs according to the sound of their past endings.*

enjoyed	watched	opened	traveled	repeated	started
helped	played	closed	visited	called	ended
needed	worked	walked	lived	discussed	washed
looked	rested	waited	asked	listened	painted

liked (t)

helped _____

loved (d)

enjoyed _____

wanted (id)

needed _____

_____   _____   _____

_____   _____   _____

_____   _____   _____

_____   _____   _____

CHAPTER FIFTEEN

Future with "going to" **Adverbs of manner**

GOING TO   Affirmative

He She	's (is)		see a movie.
I	'm (am)	going to	play tennis.
You We They	're (are)		visit Paris.

a *Write a sentence for each picture using* ***going to***.

1. _She's going to make a cake._

2. _They're going to eat dinner._

3. _____

4. _____

5. _____

6. _____

158

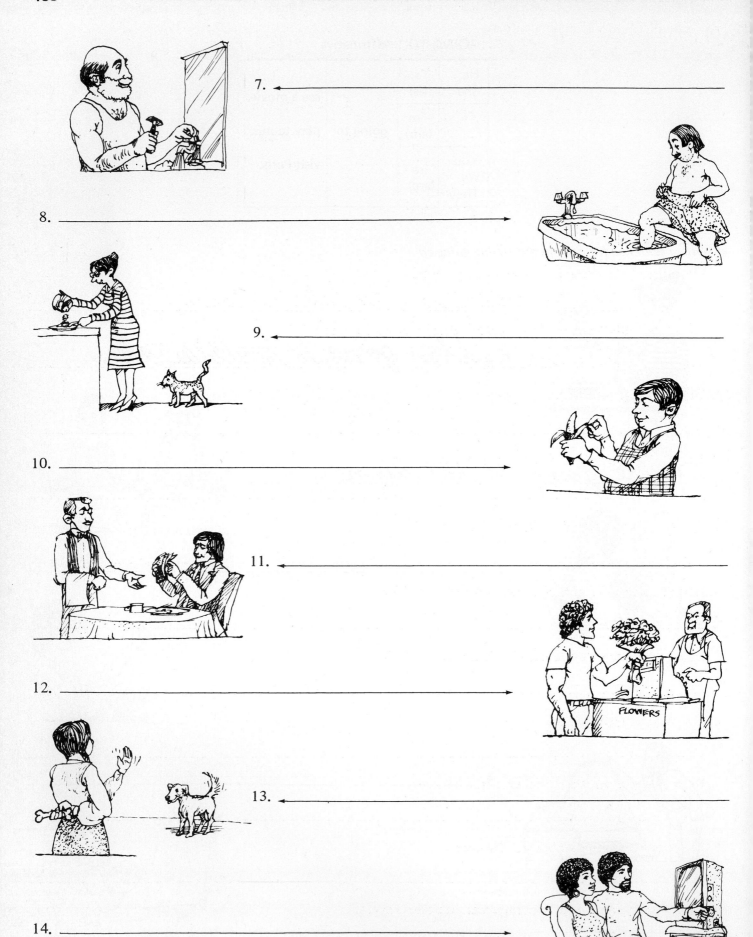

7. ←——————————————————————————————————

8. ——————————————————————————————————→

9. ←——————————————————————————————————

10. ——————————————————————————————————→

11. ←——————————————————————————————————

12. ——————————————————————————————————→

13. ←——————————————————————————————————

14. ——————————————————————————————————→

GOING TO   Negative

He She	isn't 's not (is not)		see a movie.
I	'm not (am not)	going to	play tennis.
You We They	aren't 're not (are not)		visit Paris.

b *Make negative sentences as indicated.*

Examples: They're going to take a bus.   (a taxi)

They aren't going to take a taxi.

She's going to wear her red dress.   (her blue dress)

She isn't going to wear her blue dress.

1. We're going to play tennis.   (volleyball)

_____

2. I'm going to visit my family.   (my friends)

_____

3. They're going to live in India.   (in Pakistan)

_____

4. He's going to work at the garage.   (at the post office)

_____

5. You're going to study Japanese.   (Chinese)

_____

6. I'm going to make coffee.   (tea)

_____

7. We're going to paint the kitchen.   (the bedroom)

_____

8. She's going to clean the house.   (the car)

_____

9. They're going to stop at the drugstore.   (at the market)

_____

GOING TO   Interrogative

Is	he she		see a movie?
Am	I	going to	play tennis?
Are	you we they		visit Paris?

c *Change to the interrogative.*

Examples: He's going to write a book.

Is he going to write a book?

You're going to help him.

Are you going to help him?

1. She's going to study French.

_____

2. They're going to play tennis.

_____

3. We're going to see a movie.

_____

4. He's going to work in New York.

_____

5. We're going to visit him.

_____

6. They're going to call their friends.

_____

7. She's going to make dinner.

_____

8. We're going to eat at six o'clock.

_____

9. He's going to bring his records.

_____

GOING TO   Interrogative

Is	he she		see a movie?
Am	I	going to	play tennis?
Are	you me they		visit Paris?

Short Answers

	he she	is.
Yes,	I	am.
	you we they	are.

	he she	isn't
No,	I	'm not.
	you we they	aren't.

d *Look at the pictures and answer the questions.*

1. Are Otis and Gloria going to play records?

   No, they aren't. They're going to watch TV.

2. Are Mr. and Mrs. Bascomb going to eat dinner?

   Yes, they are.

3. Is Barney going to take a shower?

   _____

4. Is Dr. Pasto going to take a book?

   _____

5. Are Jimmy and his friends going to play tennis?

_____

6. Is Tino going to buy some flowers?

_____

7. Is Anne going to call the post office?

_____

8. Are Sam and Mabel going to work in the house?

_____

9. Is Peter going to wash the car?

_____

e *Answer the following questions.*

Examples: Are you going to write a letter today?

Yes, I am. OR *No, I'm not.*

What are you going to do tomorrow?

I'm going to study at the library.

1. Can you cook?

_____

2. Are you going to make dinner tonight?

_____

3. What did you have for dinner last night?

_____

4. Where did you go yesterday?

_____

5. What did you do last weekend?

_____

6. What sports can you play?

_____

7. Where do you live?

_____

8. Do you have a big family?

_____

9. Do you watch television?

_____

10. What kind of books do you read?

_____

11. Who is your favorite actor?

_____

12. How often do you go to the movies?

_____

164

ADJECTIVES		
She's a	good bad quick slow careful	worker.

ADVERBS OF MANNER	
She works	well. badly. quickly. slowly. carefully.

f *Describe how these characters dress, run, speak, or drive.*

1. good *He dresses well.*

2. bad *He dresses badly.*

3. quick _____

4. slow _____

5. loud _____

6. soft _____

7. dangerous _____

8. careful _____

g *Look at the pictures and answer the questions.*

1. Does Mr. Bascomb speak loudly?

Yes, he does. _____

2. Does Barbara speak loudly?

No, she doesn't. She speaks softly. _____

3. Does Albert eat quickly?

_____

4. Does he run quickly?

_____

5. Do Otis and Gloria dance well?

_____

6. Does Fred dress well?

_____

7. Does he read quickly?

_____

8. Does Barney drive carefully?

_____

9. Does Jack drive carefully?

_____

10. Does Anne sing beautifully?

_____

CHAPTER SIXTEEN

Review

THERE IS/THERE ARE   Affirmative

There's (There is)	a bottle	
There are	some glasses	on the table.
There's (There is)	some money	

a   Complete the following sentences using **there's a, there's some,** or **there are some.**

Examples: *There's a* _____ pot on the stove

There's some _____ coffee in the pot.

There are some _____ cups on the shelf.

1. _____ sugar in the bowl.

2. _____ bag under the table.

3. _____ apples in the bag.

4. _____ bottle in the refrigerator.

5. _____ milk in the bottle.

6. _____ glasses on the shelf.

7. _____ handbag on the chair.

8. _____ money in the handbag.

9. _____ cigarettes next to the handbag.

10. _____ box of matches on the table.

11. _____ paper in the desk.

12. _____ pencils next to the typewriter.

b *Complete each of the following sentences with a possessive adjective or a possessive pronoun.*

Examples: Maria is looking at _____*her*_____ watch.

Give me that pen. It's _*mine*_ .

1. Do you have _____ umbrella?

2. Linda says that umbrella is _____ .

3. The Browns painted _____ house last month.

4. Peter washed _____ car this afternoon.

5. That dog belongs to Jimmy and Linda. It's _____ .

6. Barbara likes _____ job at the bank.

7. We have a new radio. But _____ television is very old.

8. That's my glass. I think you left _____ in the kitchen.

9. Can you help me? I'm looking for _____ dictionary.

10. Mr. Poole took the dictionary. He said it was _____ .

11. Did you wash _____ hair last night?

12. Mr. and Mrs. Golo paid $100 for _____ new typewriter. We got _____ for $80.

c *Write sentences about yourself using adverbs of frequency.*

Examples: usually _*I usually get up early in the morning.*_
seldom _*I seldom read the newspaper.*_

1. always _____

2. usually _____

3. often _____

4. sometimes _____

5. seldom _____

6. never _____

d *Answer the following questions about yourself.*

1. How often do you write letters?

_____

2. Who do you write to?

_____

3. Where do you study?

_____

4. Do you read quickly?

_____

5. What do you talk about with your friends?

_____

6. What kind of music do you enjoy?

_____

7. How often do you eat in restaurants?

_____

8. How often do you attend meetings?

_____

9. Are you ever in a hurry?

_____

10. Where do you go on the weekends?

_____

11. What famous person do you admire?

_____

12. Why do you admire him or her?

_____

172

PRONOUNS

Linda needs some envelopes.	She doesn't have	any.
Jimmy doesn't have any toothpaste.	He needs	some.
I need a dictionary.	I don't have	one.

e *Complete the following sentences using* **some, any,** *or* **one.**

Examples: The students need a library. They don't have ___one___.

There aren't any envelopes on the table, but there are ___some___ on the desk.

My sister got three letters last week. I didn't get ___any___.

1. Albert has two dictionaries. I only have _____.

2. Barbara needs some shampoo. She doesn't have _____.

3. Jimmy bought some records yesterday. Linda bought _____ last week.

4. They're using an old record player. We have a new _____.

5. There are two lamps in the living room. _____ is green and the other is white.

6. My girlfriend likes flowers. I'm going to take her _____ tomorrow.

7. Mrs. Hamby loves spaghetti but she can't have _____. She's watching her weight.

8. Give the chocolates to Albert. I don't want _____.

9. We don't need any milk. We already have _____.

f *Complete the following sentences with suitable prepositions.*

Example: I'm going to talk ___to___ you ___about___ Mr. and Mrs. Hamby.

1. Mr. Hamby lives _____ his wife _____ a small house _____ Maple Street.

2. They have a vegetable garden _____ their front yard.

3. There's a wire fence _____ the garden.

4. This afternoon, Mr. and Mrs. Hamby are going _____ the market.

5. The market is _____ the corner _____ Clark Street and Third Avenue.

6. Mrs. Hamby is thinking _____ the children.

7. They're walking home _____ school.

8. They're going to stop _____ the Martinoli Restaurant _____ ice cream.

OBJECT PRONOUNS

I — me	we — us
you — you	they — them
he — him	it — it
she — her	

g *Change the following sentences using object pronouns.*

Examples: Barbara bought a record <u>for Tino</u>.

She bought him a record.

I wrote a letter <u>to Mr. and Mrs. Brown</u>.

I wrote them a letter.

1. Otis gave a painting <u>to Gloria</u>.

   _____

2. We took some magazines <u>to the Browns</u>.

   _____

3. Maria made some coffee <u>for Peter</u>.

   _____

4. He got a dictionary <u>for you and me</u>.

   _____

5. Sam bought a camera <u>for Jimmy and Linda</u>.

   _____

6. He found a job <u>for Mr. Grubb</u>.

   _____

7. Simon wrote a letter <u>to his girlfriend</u>.

   _____

8. I gave some books <u>to my friends</u>.

   _____

9. They brought some chocolates <u>for you and me</u>.

   _____

10. We took some sandwiches <u>to Barney</u>.

   _____

h *Change the story about Jack Grubb to the past tense.*

Jack Grubb works at night. He has a part-time job downtown. Jack isn't married and he doesn't have a family. He lives alone in a small apartment on Bond Street. He spends most of his free time at the park across the street from his apartment. Jack goes to the park in the afternoon. He usually sits on a bench and reads the newspaper. Sometimes he meets interesting people in the park. They have conversations about all kinds of things, but most of the time they talk about sports and politics. Jack knows a lot about these subjects. He doesn't have a college education, but he's an intelligent man. He reads two or three books a week. Jack goes to the library as often as possible. There are a lot of interesting books at the public library, and it's only three blocks from Jack's apartment. But Jack's favorite place is the park. He loves the birds and the trees and the friendly people. Jack always has a good time in the park.

Jack Grubb worked at night.

i *Make original sentences with the following adverbs. Try to use a different verb for each sentence.*

Example: sadly _*She looked sadly at the photograph.*_

1. quickly _____

2. well _____

3. badly _____

4. slowly _____

5. happily _____

6. carefully _____

7. terribly _____

8. beautifully _____

9. softly _____

j *Complete the following sentences.*

Example: Last Sunday _*I went to the beach.*_

1. My sister is popular because _____

2. When I need help I _____

3. Do you think _____

4. We often talk about _____

5. I get mad when _____

6. Tomorrow _____

7. Why do you _____

8. There aren't any _____

9. In my free time I often _____

10. Yesterday afternoon _____

11. When are you going to _____

12. Most people _____

13. I'm sorry _____

14. What did you _____

k *Make questions using **who, what, when,** or **where**.*

Examples: Albert visited the Browns last weekend. *Who did he visit last weekend?*

He showed them his new dictionary. *What did he show them?*

He got it at the bookstore on Maple Street. *Where did he get it?*

1. Barney called Nancy this morning. _____

2. He told her an interesting story. _____

3. It was about some people from San Francisco. _____

4. He met them at the airport last night. _____

5. They wore cowboy hats. _____

6. Barney took them to the Wickam Restaurant. _____

7. They arrived at ten o'clock. _____

8. Barney had dinner with his new friends. _____

9. They talked about movies. _____

10. They left the restaurant at twelve o'clock. _____

11. They went to a hotel on Main Street. _____

l *Write original sentences using the following words and expressions.*

Example: finally *She finally found her keys.*

1. alone _____

2. summer _____

3. unfortunately _____

4. on time _____

5. this weekend _____

6. last night _____

7. weather _____

8. a lot of _____

9. except _____

10. before _____

m *Peter Smith is on vacation in the South Pacific. On Friday, July 9th, he writes a letter to his friend, Otis, in California. As you can see, he is very happy.*

Friday, July 9.

Dear Otis,

I'm writing to you from Paradise Island. This is a wonderful place for a vacation. They have good food, beautiful beaches, and sunny weather. I'm staying at the Sunset Hotel. It's not expensive and the service is excellent. The people are very friendly here. I hope you're having a good time in California. See you in a couple of weeks.

Take care,
Peter

A week later, Peter writes another letter to Otis. This time he isn't very happy. Complete Peter's letter.

Friday, July 16.

Dear Otis,
I'm writing to you...

n *Write a short composition about what you did last weekend.*

_____

_____

_____

_____

_____

_____

_____

_____

_____

_____

_____

_____